Days in
Spring

Vic Parker

Raintree

Chicago, Illinois

Printed and bound by South China Printing Company.
07 06 05
10 9 8 7 6 5 4 3 2 1

Library of Congress Cataloging-in-Publication Data:
Parker, Victoria.
 Spring / Victoria Parker.
     v. cm. — (Days in)
Includes index.
Contents: It's springtime! — Nature trail — At the stream — Farm
babies — Hungry horses — Buy a pet — Busy in the garden — Teddy
bears' picnic — Pond dipping — Easter fun.
 ISBN 1-4109-0736-8 (lib. bdg. : hardcover) — ISBN 1-4109-0741-4
(pbk.)
 1. Spring—Juvenile literature. [1. Spring.] I. Title.
 QB637.5.P37 2004
 508.2—dc22
                        2003019843

Acknowledgments
The publisher would like to thank the following for permission to reproduce photographs: p. 4 Getty Images, pp. 11
(David Woodfall), p. 21 (Nicki Pardo); p. 5 Trevor Clifford; pp. 6, 18, 23 Steve Behr/Stockpile; p. 7 (top) Ardea (C. Jack
& A. Bailey); p. 7 (bottom) Zefa (M. Botek); pp. 8-9 Alamy (Peter Usbeck); p. 10 Imagestate; pp. 12-13 Gareth Boden;
p. 14 Angela Hampton; p. 15 Martin Sookias; p. 16 Corbis, pp. 17, 19, 22 (Ariel Skelley); p. 20 Cornish Picture Library;
p. 21 Science Photo Library (Claude Nuridsany & Marie Perennou)

Cover photograph reproduced with permission of Zefa/L. Buechner

Every effort has been made to contact copyright holders of any material reproduced in this book.
Any omissions will be rectified in subsequent printings if notice is given to the publishers.

Some words are shown in bold, **like this**. You can find out
what they mean by looking in the glossary on page 24.

Contents

It's Springtime!

Trees and plants are growing.

4

Nature Trail

What can you spot on a spring walk?

Look up high.
Birds nest among branches.

Look down low.
Ladybugs live among leaves.

7

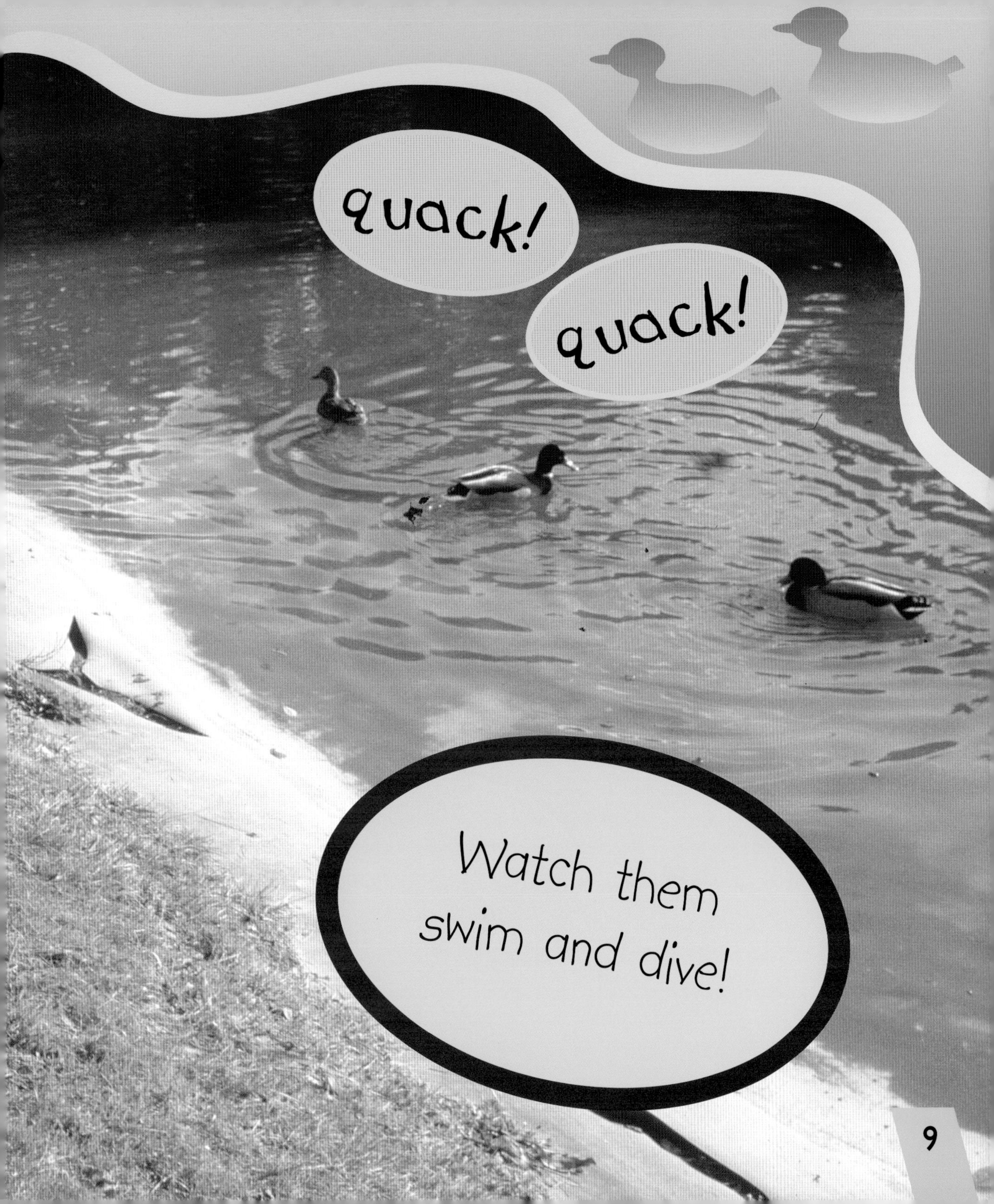

Watch them swim and dive!

Farm Babies

Lots of farm animals have babies in the spring.

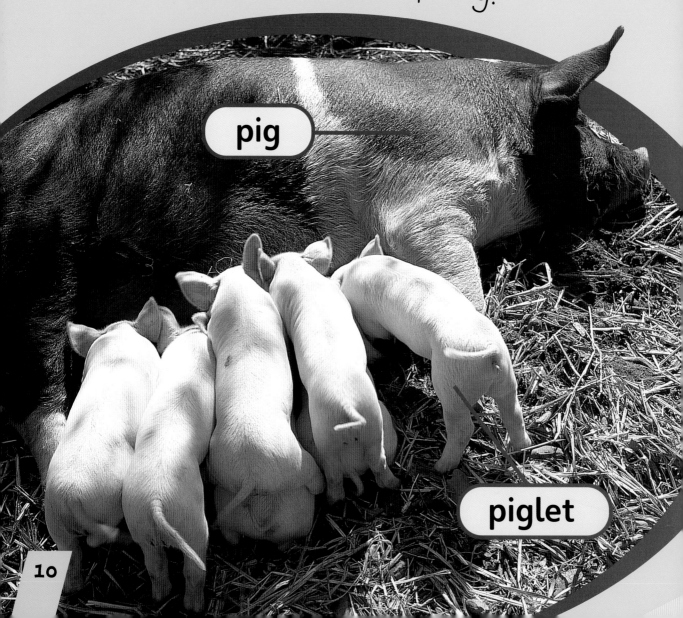

pig

piglet

lamb

Hungry Horses

Take some apples for the horse to **munch** and **crunch**.

Baby horses are called **foals**.

Do you know what rabbits like to eat?

Busy in the Garden

Spring is a good time to grow things in the garden.

Plant some **seedlings** in a row,
water them and watch
them grOW.

Teddy Bears' Picnic

It is fun to take
your teddy into
the yard for
a picnic treat.

At the Pond

At the pond,
creatures
swim and
crawl
and hop
everywhere.

Mother's Day

We give gifts on mother's day.

Glossary

foal a baby horse

seedling tiny plant that has just come out of a seed

Index

Notes for adults

The *Days in...* series helps young children become familiar with the way their environment changes through the year. The books explore the natural world in each season and how this affects community life and social activities. The books also focus on celebrations, which are particular to certain times of the year. Used together, the books will enable discussion about similarities and differences between the seasons.

This book introduces the reader to the season of spring. It will encourage young children to think about spring weather, wildlife and landscape and activities they can enjoy in spring. The book will help children extend their vocabulary, as they will hear new words such as *foal* and *seedling*.

Additional information about the seasons
Not all places in the world have four seasons. Climate is affected by two factors: 1) how near a place is to the Equator (hence how much heat it receives from the Sun), 2) how high a place is (mountains are cooler than nearby lowlands). This is why some parts of the world have just two seasons, such as the hot wet season and the hot dry season across much of India. Other parts of the world have just one season, such as the year-long heat of the Sahara desert or the year-long cold of the North Pole.

Follow-up activities
• Draw a picture of a woodland scene in spring, with insects, animals, birds and people.
• Take a trip to a library to find out more about Easter and the spring festivals of other cultures.
• Dress up as spring animals and insects by making masks.